AUSTRALIAN TERRIER

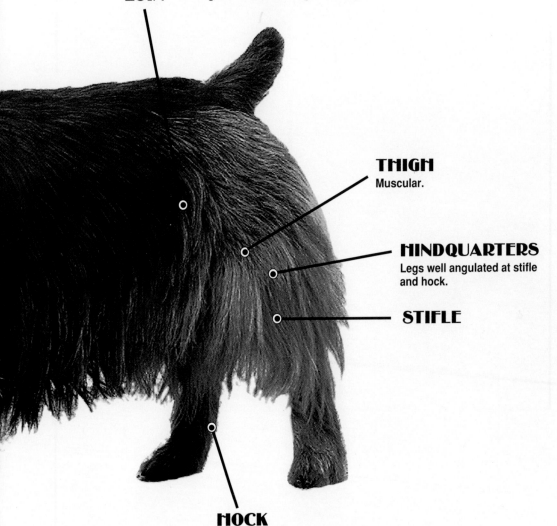

LOIN — Strong and short with slight tuck-up.

THIGH
Muscular.

HINDQUARTERS
Legs well angulated at stifle and hock.

STIFLE

HOCK

Title page: Standing ovation for the Australian Terrier, photographed by Isabelle Francais. Owner, Alexa Samarotto.

Photographers: Animal World Studio, David Ashbey, John L. Ashbey, Martin Booth, Brandon Studios, Inc., William Brown, Joseph A. Cirincione, Cott/Francis Photography, Isabelle Francais, William P. Gilbert, Terence A. Gili, Graham Studios, Bernard W. & W. Kay Kernan, Mikron Photos, Ltd., Olson Photo, Don Petrulis, Perry Phillips Photography, Tobé Saskor Photography, Vince Serbin, Evelyn M. Shafer, Chuck and Sandy Tatham.

Dedication

This book is dedicated to the memory of my husband, Milton Fox

Distributed in the UNITED STATES to the Pet Trade by T.F.H. Publications, Inc., One T.F.H. Plaza, Neptune City, NJ 07753; distributed in the UNITED STATES to the Bookstore and Library Trade by National Book Network, Inc. 4720 Boston Way, Lanham MD 20706; in CANADA to the Pet Trade by H & L Pet Supplies Inc., 27 Kingston Crescent, Kitchener, Ontario N2B 2T6; Rolf C. Hagen Inc., 3225 Sartelon St. Laurent-Montreal Quebec H4R 1E8; in CANADA to the Book Trade by Vanwell Publishing Ltd., 1 Northrup Crescent, St. Catharines, Ontario L2M 6P5 ; in ENGLAND by T.F.H. Publications, PO Box 15, Waterlooville PO7 6BQ; in AUSTRALIA AND THE SOUTH PACIFIC by T.F.H. (Australia), Pty. Ltd., Box 149, Brookvale 2100 N.S.W., Australia; in NEW ZEALAND by Brooklands Aquarium Ltd. 5 McGiven Drive, New Plymouth, RD1 New Zealand; in Japan by T.F.H. Publications, Japan—Jiro Tsuda, 10-12-3 Ohjidai, Sakura, Chiba 285, Japan; in SOUTH AFRICA by Lopis (Pty) Ltd., P.O. Box 39127, Booysens, 2016, Johannesburg, South Africa. Published by T.F.H. Publications, Inc.

MANUFACTURED IN THE
UNITED STATES OF AMERICA
BY T.F.H. PUBLICATIONS, INC.

AUSTRALIAN TERRIER

TERRIER

A COMPLETE AND RELIABLE HANDBOOK

Nell Fox

RX-107

ABOUT THE AUTHOR

Author Nell Fox at around ten years of age with her first Australian Terrier, "Punch." Photograph taken in New Zealand around 1910. Mrs. Fox enjoyed the company of Australian Terriers while she lived in New Zealand and, with her husband Milton, was the first to import them into the United States in the 1940s. She is recognized as a Founder of the Australian Terrier Club of America, for which she served as Secretary, Delegate and Director for many years. Her highly regarded first book *How to Raise and Train an Australian Terrier*, on which this current publication is based, was issued by T.F.H. in 1965. Today it is a valued collector's item. In 1994 the officers and directors of the Australian Terrier Club of America bestowed upon Mrs. Fox the title of Lifetime Patroness of the Australian Terrier Club of America for her lifetime dedication to the breed. In 1997, she was further honored for her 50 years as a breeder, exhibitor and prominent club member. Mrs. Fox still lives at her Pleasant Pasture Kennels in Point Pleasant, New Jersey with her beloved Aussies, and her name continues to be associated with the top dogs in the country. Currently she has bred well over 200 AKC champions.

CONTENTS

The Australian Terrier that made Mrs. Fox the most proud: Aust-Can-Col-Ber-Mex-Am-Int. Ch. Tinee Town Talkbac, ROM, a.k.a. "Joey," winner of 180 Bests of Breed, 84 Group placements and 4 Bests in Show. Joey sired 46 champions.

DESCRIPTION OF THE AUSTRALIAN TERRIER

"Grand Little Dogs" is an apt description for Australian Terriers. Big in nature, small in stature, they are among the smallest members of the Terrier Group. The standard specifies size as "average 12–14 pounds," so the actual size of each individual will vary somewhat.

The coat should be harsh and straight, about 2 1/2 inches long, with a short, soft undercoat. The soft topknot, which protects the eyes when burrowing, and the neck ruff, which is meant to be a protective feature when hunting, are definite Aussie character-

Ch. Regency Lord of Summerhill, owned by Ida Ellen Weinstock and Alice Ann Wight and bred by Cathy Lester.

Ch. Plesantpastures Tak-A-Chance, CD and Ch. Tammikins Waggedy Andy, CD, CG are owned by Susan Saulvester.

DESCRIPTION

istics. The color may be blue or silver-black with golden tones on the head and legs, or the whole coat may be clear red or sandy colored.

Though anxious to participate in all activities and exceedingly fun-loving, an Aussie responds quickly to the mood of his owner, whether it is to play, to walk, to ride in the car, or perhaps to have a lesson in obedience training (to which the breed responds better than most other terriers). He is equally delighted to snuggle on his master's slippers or his mistress's lap, or to cuddle with someone nearer his own size.

There is a natural attraction between youngsters and Aussies. Those who have had their childhood enriched with the companionship of an Australian Terrier will always do their utmost to see that their own children have the joy of growing up with such a delightful, loyal "cobber" (the word for "pal" in Australia).

The description "one-man dog" is somewhat loosely applied, as it can have various meanings to different people, and if it is interpreted when applied to Aussies to mean that only one person can win an affectionate response, that is not so. Though an Aussie will frequently attach himself to one person, no normal Aussie will be nasty to other people. It is typical of the breed to be close and affectionate with the whole family, though he usually attaches himself rather specially to one family member. Usually outsiders are treated politely, but without gush.

Aussies, like the ever-loyal "Zeal" owned and loved by Janet Repp, make affectionate and dedicated pets.

Mary M. O'Connell, protected by her three favorite Aussies: Ch. Shewme's Debrickasaw, Ch. Franjoy's Colin's Hot Pursuit and Ch. Seadog's Rosie O'Grady.

The watchdog instinct is deeply embedded in the Australian Terrier, but this does not tend toward his having a yappy or snappish disposition. An Aussie will bark at unusual sounds or at a stranger, but with a little training will accept the intrusion as soon as he knows his people are aware of what is happening. Receiving proper understanding, affection, and consideration, an Aussie seldom wanders from home. It is usual for them to enjoy the company of other dogs and live happily with breeds of all sizes, and also with other kinds of animals.

Aussies are terriers through and through. Dancer and her Smooth Fox Terrier buddy are exploring a burrow. In order to earn the CG (Certificate of Gameness), terriers must prove their ability to go to ground after quarry. Owner, Esther C. Krom.

DESCRIPTION

Three foundation Aussies in America: Ch. Elvyne Regal Salute, CDX, Best of Breed at Westminster in 1959 and 1960 over record-breaking entries; Ch. Elvyne Blue Taffeta, dam of the first champion; and Willelva Wanderer, CD, the first Aussie to gain the Companion Dog title.

BEGINNINGS OF THE AUSSIE

Toward the end of the nineteenth century, the busy newcomers to Australia needed a dog that could share their rugged lives—one who would help guard their homes and gold mines, who would control varmints, and who could withstand both the hot summers and wet, windy winters. Along with these qualities, they also wanted to add companionship, affection, and loyalty to their comparatively lonely lives. As with other pioneers, with prosperity came the desire for not only a rough little dog but also one sufficiently good-looking to grace the seats of their carriages and the hearths of their homes. The very same functions that endeared the breed to his native country are practically the same in America, because the vast territory in the USA, with its countless climatic changes,

Left: Ch. Elvyne Regal Salute, CDX was the first English import and the first Aussie CDX, sent to Mrs. Fox by Miss E. Swyer. Right: Ch. Tinee Town Traveller, imported by Mrs. Fox, was a multiple Best of Breed winner and the brother to the famous Tinee Town Tip Toes.

offers so many needs to which a dog must respond. For example, there are areas in America where families depend on an Aussie's warning and protection against snakes entering the children's playground. These functions seem just as, if not more, necessary today than ever before, and the Aussie's highly developed sense of hearing adds to his instinctive watchdog qualities. In the past and now, loyalty and love are desired in a dog, and the equally active lives of the pioneers and present-day Americans call for a conveniently sized dog that requires minimum grooming, eats economically, and is known for his longevity and intelligence. So over the years, as these various requirements presented themselves, a few crosses with other terriers were made.

The Australian Terrier is the happy result of man's knowledge and ingenuity combined with the best he and Nature had already produced in the breeding of the British short-legged sporting terriers. All credit goes to the Australian breeders who undertook the difficult task of establishing from the limited sources available in Australia a breed appropriate for their own needs and locale. The terms Broken-coated Terrier (signifying a double coat) and Rough Terrier identified

Cooees Straleon Anzac, CD (sired by Willelva Wanderer out of Elvyne Blue Taffeta) was a special pal of the author's husband, Milton Fox.

the breed that developed into the Australian Terrier (Rough Terrier was the name used in the indexes of Australian dog books until 1897). In 1864, Australia held its first dog show. About 20 years later, dog shows presented classes for Broken-coated Terriers over or under 7 pounds, and these were further divided by color: blue, sandy, and any color other than blue or sandy.

With her puppy, this is Ch. Tinee Town Tip Toes, affectionately known as "Wriggles," an import to Pleasant Pastures Kennels in the early 1960s.

FURTHER BREED IMPROVEMENT

The first Australian Terrier club was formed in 1887. Australian Rough Terriers were exhibited about two years before, at Melbourne shows. From this period, for about 30 years, various sturdy, sporting, short-legged terriers were crossed for special improvements. Although somewhat the same type of terrier was shown in Scotland in 1880, a distinctly different breed was finally fixed "Down Under." The Australians started with dogs brought from the British

Ch. Tinee Town Tip Toes was a blue/tan import who won many Bests of Breed at distinguished shows in America. Sired by Seven Oaks Woodpecker out of Seven Oaks Sweetheart, she was bred by Mrs. Pat Connors of Victoria, Australia.

Isles by the early settlers, who evidently realized, though they had in these first Australian Terriers a sound basis, it was necessary to seek improvement with well-considered cross-breedings. These first Australian Terrier breeders had an advantage and took the opportunity of developing the best from the already established small terriers. Because of the size of the Antipodes, with its defined geographic divisions, and the lack of leading breeding kennels and control councils as we know them today, registrations, regulations, and records were not strictly followed. Nevertheless, there are sufficient reports to

Cooees Straleon Idle, owned by Mr. and Mrs. Milton Fox.

DESCRIPTION

Charles Deer handles Ch. Seven Oaks Silver Lining to Best of Breed and John Whalen handles Ch. Plesantpastures Janet Jill to Best of Opposite at the 1964 National Specialty. Judge, John T. Marvin.

determine that the ancestry of the Australian Terrier is made up from the Dandie Dinmont Terrier (for protective and decorative topknots), the prick-eared Skye Terrier (for ear carriage, litheness, length of body, neck ruff, and front coat apron to help guard these vulnerable parts), a small Irish Terrier, perhaps the Manchester Terrier (for enriching the color), and the Scottish Terrier, which differed somewhat from today's Scottie (for the harsh, weatherproof coat). To retain a conveniently small size and to emphasize pleasant color, the Yorkshire Terrier was introduced, and probably again for erect ears and coat quality, the Cairn Terrier was used. The coloring of the Lakeland Terrier, then known as the Patterdale, is reminiscent of some Aussies, but there is no known crossing with

Ch. Plesantpastures Tru Freckles as a youngster. Bred by Mrs. Fox.

these three latter breeds and Australian Terriers were a firmly established breed in Australia, as we have already proven, by the time the Norwich Terrier could have reached there. The similarity between Aussies and other small working terriers is the result of their mutual ancestry. To emphasize the secure and fixed composition of the Australian Terrier, there is the fact that other breeds used Australian Terriers for improvement in and establishment of their breeds. This was done by the Silky Terrier, whose standard was drawn up in 1909 in Australia, which is evidence that Australian Terriers were so firmly established by then that fanciers of new breeds did not hesitate to use them.

Mrs. Fox visits Australia in 1968 to be greeted by a parade of Aussies in her honor.

THE AUSSIE IN OTHER COUNTRIES

Naturally most of the Australian Terriers first exhibited in America were imports. Some were champions from Australia, New Zealand, England, and Ireland. In July 1960, the American Kennel Club officially recognized the Australian Terrier. Many years previous, Australian Terriers had been recognized in Australasia, India, South Africa, Canada, Ireland, and England. British interest and consequent admiration were heightened by the Henham Kennels' Australian Terriers owned by the Earl of Stadbroke who, upon returning to England in 1926 from his term as Governor General of Australia, brought with him some Aussies. Enthusiasm for the breed was again fanned by the Duke of Gloucester in 1934 when, upon returning from the same position, he brought Australian Terriers with him. He renewed his interest in the breed upon his 1945 visit to Australia and he continued to breed Aussies for many years. The Australian Terrier Club of England was founded about 1933 when the English Kennel Club officially recognized the breed.

Distinguished terrier authority Charles Deer with Ch. Tinee Town Traveller. Mr. Deer worked for years with Mrs. Fox to help establish the breed in the U.S. He showed many of Nell's dogs to great wins, and became a renowned AKC judge.

THE AUSSIE IN AMERICA

No definite date can be marked for the arrival of Australian Terriers in America. It is known that in 1900 one came from Australia and lived until 1923! Soldiers from World Wars I and II were responsible for bringing in many Aussies, as were numerous travelers who also brought some from England and Ireland. There are references to the breed being present on Long Island during mid 1940s. In the mid- and late 1950s, a small but enthusiastic group of Australian Terrier fanciers was working for the breed's successful, speedy progress in the United States.

Until a breed is allowed entrance into the Stud Book of the American Kennel Club, which comes with official AKC recognition, it has to be shown in the Miscellaneous Class. At the 1957 Westminster Ken-

At Westminster in 1959, Mrs. Fox won with NZ-Aus-Am. Ch. Merryvale Suzette under the great international judge Percy Roberts.

nel Club show in New York the seven Aussies shown drew enthusiastic spectators, as did the nine shown in 1958. The 44 entries in 1959 and the 58 entries in 1960 in the Miscellaneous Class broke all such entry records. It was the press and public expressing such keen delight for the breed that secured its future in the US, and truthfully the world over.

In April 1957 in New York City, the Australian Terrier Club of America held its first meeting, and soon after became incorporated. This club's first specialty show was in New York in 1962, with an encouraging entry of 51 Australian Terriers. Now the Australian Terrier Club is actively functioning with hundreds of members and sponsoring many AKC dog shows and sanctioned matches as well as its own specialties.

In all English-speaking countries, Aussies are valued, loving members of families as well as adaptable little working terriers. Australia and the US are the leading countries for both breed quantity and quality. Long-time breeders continue to breed typical and top-rated specimens. Denmark, Brazil, and France were among the first Continental countries to acquire these handsome terriers, and others followed with enthusiasm. Today Australian Terriers are imported and exported to and from many countries.

Wonga Rhon Ginger Snap of Pleasant Pastures was a blue and tan import from the renowned Seven Oaks Kennels in Victoria, Australia.

At the 1968 National, Koriella's Robinson, bred by Mrs. Annemarie Lowe and owned by Mrs. Fox, was Best of Breed, and Plesantpastures Idle Talk, bred and owned by Mrs. Fox, was Best of Opposite.

Being a devoted companion, guarding against trespassers, and hunting rodents are among the most important functions required of terriers, and Aussies fulfill all of these demands splendidly. Young and old delight in the warm, intelligent responses to people's moods, whatever the surroundings may be and in any kind of climatic condition. Being bright, alert, and devoted, Australian Terriers are unsurpassed as pals. The future of these all-purpose "Down Under darlings" in America continues to be promising and happy, and they indeed remain "Grand Little Dogs."

Ch. Wonga Rhon Freckles, owned by Mrs. Cora Nathan, winning at Westminster in 1962 under Gen. Edward B. McKinley.

THE AUSSIE COMES OF AGE

Mrs. E. Williams of the Willelva Kennels in Australia sent many great dogs to America, and the author is fortunate to have known and worked with this great breeder of days gone by. Mrs. Williams passed along an unpublished manuscript dedicated "to the most intelligent and lovable of all breeds," and we are fortunate to present portions of this insightful script to our readers. Although penned over 30 years ago, this previously unpublished book contains much wisdom and insight that are as timely and pertinent today as they were when the great lady wrote them.

Willelva pups at four months old. Bred by Mrs. E. Williams; their dam was Willelva Janannie.

My first introduction to the Australian Terrier was in 1949 when I bought Barolday Terry-Boy from the Barolday Kennels at the age of six weeks. He had been in his first show and with him I was handed his first red, white and blue sash for best baby pup and a first-prize certificate, of which I was very proud. This meant little to me at the time because I had not yet started showing. Terry-Boy went to the top among the Aussies many times and I wanted to shout with pride and joy to the whole street when he got a blue ribbon at his first Royal Easter show at the age of six months. It was my first Royal show experience and I will never forget it. It was a pouring wet day; I had no transport so I had to put my dog in a dog box and take him in a tram, then walk over to the RAS show grounds. We couldn't wait to get out of the rain, and I had to have the dog benched by 8:15 a.m. So like drowned rats, we trudged on through the ground, waited to get through the vetting, and found the bench. Then after all the excitement, the schedule was changed and we were not taken until near the last on account of the rain. The showing had to take place inside the pavilion. This meant a long wait, and what with the noise of the rain on the iron roof, the shouting, barking, crowding, I thought, "This is the first and last show for me," and so did Terry-Boy. By the time the Aussies were shown, being a highly strung breed, full of pep, he was at the end of his tether and I did not expect him to do his best. This was the first time I had handled a dog before a big crowd, and being indoors coupled with the noise of the deluge on the roof, and before an English judge (Leo Wilson), I'm afraid all my practice went to the wind! Mr. Wilson was a sport, tolerant, and took into consideration the circumstances. He saw

Mrs. Fox visiting with Pat Connor in Victoria in 1967. Tinee Town Jennie sits on Pat's lap and Daisey sits with Nell. Daisey was imported to the States by Nell after this visit.

that my dog was good, though badly handled, but after parading him several times, awarded him the blue ribbon. We proceeded to the open class to win a third place. I never lost the thrill of my first Royal and I hope that this retelling will give someone the encouragement to keep trying.

Arriving home on this auspicious day, tired out, with my aching but proud head, I threw my hat on the bed and was enjoying a cup of tea, when upon hearing a noise, I investigated to find my hat on the carpet with Terry rolling all over it. He paused and peered up at me with a wicked look as if to say, "That's been with me all day and now I've had my revenge." The hat never made it to another show, though we sure did.

In his show career, Terry brought home many Bests of Breeds: sashes, cups and trophies. My greatest pride is his championship award card that he

Barolday Topsy, a red bitch with a litter of puppies. Owned by Mrs. E. Williams of Willelva Kennels in Randwick, Australia.

gained at an early age, and never at small shows. He loved opposition in more ways than showing, for his spirit knew no bounds. He had the honor of being the first Aussie in New South Wales to win a Group, so at least some of his achievements go down in history. He actually had the points to gain the Grand Championship, but I never applied for it.

He sired the first Aussie to gain a championship in America, has sired several champions in Australia and the USA. He was a wonderful companion, a fearless fighter, yet able to be handled and subdued, loved by all who knew him.

We added a dear little red bitch called Barolday Topsy. She was one of the prettiest Aussies I think I have ever seen and of a glorious color. She gave my sister show interest and won many awards and sashes. She was Terry's mate in every way. Not only did they give us some fine red litters, but they were team mates. She was always at the back of him in all their hunting pursuits. Once they got a hint of mice or rats, nothing would hold them back. One day they found a hole in the ground underneath a huge aviary. They dug until finally they disturbed a nest of rats. As fast as Terry would haul one out and throw it over his head, Topsy was there to catch and finish it off. Then she would push him to one side, as if to say, "Give me a go," and so they went until they got every one.

Nell Fox with 1962 Specialty winner Ch. Seven Oaks True Story, one of the great Seven Oaks imports to establish the breed in the U.S.

Our dear little Susan, Seven Oaks Blue Smoke, was a clever show dog and a born actress—never have I seen such a perfect actress when she got into the ring—she really played to an audience. A clever mother and entertainer, she left some champions behind her, many of whom brought forth famous American Aussies.

I'm quite sure it's personal love and interest that develops into that devoted affection and faithfulness. I could not record all the tales I have been told about the little dogs bought from our kennel, which is the reward we like best.

We have sold many to farmers, who say they are very clever at bringing in the cows. Another of our dogs, Lance, was trained to the gun to retrieve with great success.

One little red bitch, the smallest of a litter, went to Bathurst and became famous as a snake-killer. One day her master stepped out of his door almost onto a snake, but Tiny saw it and killed it with one swoop before his master's astonished eyes. On another occasion, Tiny pounced upon a large black snake that was ready to strike a child's leg. She was quick to act and bashed the snake to the ground.

Her master and mistress were artists, and as such traveled around a bit. One Sunday her mistress had settled herself on a log with her sketching block and her master had just set up his easel nearby, when Tiny saw a tiger snake crawling along the ground against the log. Had her mistress moved even a muscle, the snake would have attacked. Tiny, at a disadvantage on the opposite side, knew to act quickly. She sprang and grabbed it, but its fangs went into her neck. She hung on and the snake was terribly mauled and died, but Tiny, her owners could see, was in a bad way

Ch. Plesantpastures Wags Noble, handled by Mrs. Fox, under Glen Fancy at the 1969 National.

herself. She gave them a look to say, "I did my duty." They rushed her to the vet, but it was too late. That brave little dog had already killed at least twelve snakes, and finally gave her life for her beloved mistress.

I have no doubt that other Aussie people could tell many tales such as these. All think that their own dogs are special, and why not! Each has endeared himself by some habit or memory that will live forever with his owners. Maybe he or she was a rascal, but the loving owner could always find an excuse for him.

Milton and Nell Fox enjoying the company of their Aussies at Pleasant Pasture Kennel in the early 1960s. In America, the Foxes are regarded as the Aussie's first family.

PLEASANT PASTURES IN AMERICA

Australian Terriers enjoyed popularity in Australia, their homeland, New Zealand and Ireland, as well as India, Africa, Denmark and Canada. Although by the '50s some had been imported into America, it was not until Mrs. Milton Fox of Pleasant Pasture Kennels, New Jersey, who incidentally had owned them years ago when she lived in New Zealand, once more became interested that they were brought before the public eye and made popular. Mrs. Fox imported from England, and in 1956 I sold her a blue and tan dog,

Willie, formally Willelva Wanderer, CD, proved his value as a terrier by killing this Kingsnake in a matter of seconds.

Willelva Wanderer, a son of Terry-Boy, who would become the absolute darling of her heart. These first English import and Willie (as she called him) gave Mrs. Fox her earnest start in Aussies. She became famous all over America and Canada for her dogs. In 1957 Willelva Kennels sent her two red bitch puppies, Jannanie and Weja, both Aboriginal names meaning "Ours" and "To Love," respectively.

Willie, Nell Fox's first love, encouraged her growing in interest in the breed. Full of energy and spirit, he gave Nell and her husband Milton some happy moments. On one occasion he jumped into the fish pond and ate the fish, and on another he followed their Collie out into the snow and got lost. But it was not that long until he proved his worth by killing two huge snakes.

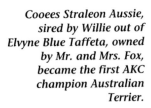

Cooees Straleon Aussie, sired by Willie out of Elvyne Blue Taffeta, owned by Mr. and Mrs. Fox, became the first AKC champion Australian Terrier.

At this time the Australian Terrier had not been recognized by the AKC, but nothing daunted Mrs. Fox and she worked untiringly to achieve this goal. She entered her dogs in the Miscellaneous Classes as well as obedience classes. Willie was the first of his breed to earn the CD obedience title, probably the first in the world to receive such a title.

Willie became the sire of the first American champion, Cooees Straleon Aussie out of Elvyne Blue Taffeta, an English import and Wanderer's first love, a fine bitch who has made her name famous— Merryvale Suzette from the Merryvale Kennel—all these dogs brought fame to Pleasant Pastures. Mrs Fox is largely heralded as the proponent for the breed's recognition and popularity in the USA.

Ch. Cooees Straleon Bracider, UD, owned by Mrs. Augusta Evanuk.

THE AUSSIE COMES OF AGE

In 1959 Mrs. Bywater of Seven Oaks Kennels in Victoria took ten champions to America, where she was the guest of Mrs. Fox for some time. Mrs. Fox acquired some of these and bred them with her own champion stock. Following these were Tinee Town Traveller and Tinee Town Tip Toes, the former was a beautiful breed representative who proved his value and the latter sent his happy companion, became even more famous.

In 1961 Mr. and Mrs. Milton Fox received the Dog Breeders of the Year award for their work in establishing the Australian Terrier. Willelva Kennels were proud of their share in helping to establish Mrs. Fox's kennels.

Two of Mrs. Fox's favorites, Willelva Wanderer, CD and NZ-Aus-Am. Ch. Merryvale Suzette, bred by Mrs. J. Vignes in 1954, both produced outstanding offspring.

MRS. FOX'S FIRST AND FAVORITE

Willie

Mrs. Fox writes to her first great Aussie:

My darling Miscellaneous Ch. Willelva Wanderer CD, how much we have learned to love you, how much we have learned from you. It is a sad heart that realizes that you—the dad, granddad, and great-granddad—will never be able to share the joys that are to come our way. You may be an AKC number, but never will you sit on our benches, never will you be in the spotlight, never, except in our hearts where you will always be "the wonderful one."

Your ears, so wonderful, so predominately yours, are carried high and erect ever proudly by Pinedale's Inune of Wollongong. Your rich blue-tan colored coat is worn anew on Sheslie's Rewa Clearfield. Can it be concealed that, as I lead Cooees Straleon Aussie of Pleasant Pastures in the ring, the gait, the strut is the same as yours? Your very eyes seem to be looking up at me through the eyes of Stonebrae's Seven Oaks Wendy. His intelligence, his alertness remind me of what a superb little hunter you used to be—the enemy of every snake, rabbit and rat in the countryside. You go to shows with us now in piece and parts, all these lovable features in different carrying cases. But this is the way of the world. And we love you even more.

Tinee Town Talewagger, ROM and Ch. Tinee Town Telltale winning at Westminster in 1967. Owned by Mrs. Fox and bred by Mrs. Pat Connor.

It is with a sad heart that we desert you at home, taking youngsters to Philadelphia, Westminster, Washington and Chicago. You will not be an American champion when we get to show in the Group: recog-

nition comes too late. But I know there are many "Willies": some live well; others merely live. Some leave at their death the memory of an extraordinary life, a memory that, instead of fading, grows stronger year after year. Each succeeding generation cries from its quivering nose to its wagging tail: "I am Willie... I am Willie."

Stay with us, Willie, a little longer; sleep on the foot of the bed. Your eyes have been dimmed, but a thousand lights gleam behind them. There will never be an Australian Terrier bench not the better for having had you somewhere in the past, and difficult as it may be to take consolation from it now, you will always be on that bench, alive in the furthest future.

A tribute to Joey: Aus-Can-Col-Ber-Mex-Am-Int. Ch. Tinee Town Talkbac, ROM winning the Stud Dog class with Ch. Plesantpastures Ma's Jubilee and Ch. Plesantpastures Ma's Jason under judge Mrs. Thelma Brown.

Joey

Mrs. Fox reminisces about one of the breed greats:
When emotions are so deep, so strong, it seems words to describe them are as impossible to grasp as water from a fresh spring, but my feeling about Joey are as powerful as the waterfall that feeds the spring.

From the moment Joey stepped out, undaunted, ears, tail up, after 96 hours of travel in his Australian crate, I knew one of the greatest Australian Terriers had come to America and into my life. Time proved the truth of that first impression of the summer of 1971. Following exploratory sniffs at his new surroundings, he came confidently to me and looked up trustingly into my eyes. Instantly a mutual bond of faith and communication was established. Charles Deer, a terrier expert, and I were instantly enthralled. We were sure of Joey's unique greatness because he possessed a sparking personality, with intelligence, reliability and a warmth within a body that presented

all the physical correctness and confidence we had ever hoped to see in an Aussie. In July of that summer, Charles Deer took Joey to his first Group win under Robert Graham, and made quite a splash as the Aussie was still a "new" breed in the US in the early '70s.

Proving the truth of our first impression, consider the grand little record of Australian Terrier Aust-Can-Col-Ber-Mex-Am-Int. Ch. Tinee Town Talkbac, ROM—Joey, to all of us, and the sire of 46 AKC champions and the winner of 4 Bests in Show, 29 Group firsts, and 54 other Group placement during his short life in America.

The first of Joey's great Best in Show victories was on February 26, 1972 in Providence, RI under judge Mr. Bresnahan and handled by Charles Deer.

He lived in the house with me and soon became my loving companion. When Joey arrived I had been a widow many years. Not only did he bring cheer to me but he became the dear pal of my other Aussies. However, his favorite was my Jenny, at that time, the top-winning bitch in the US. Joey had good taste! He loudly announced trespassers but was never belligerent with people and quite sociable with my friends. Never aggressive to other dogs, however, he bristled up if one started anything.

There was an occasion when I had to show Joey myself at a big show where a top-winning dog with a well-known professional handler would be the main competition. I was naturally nervous. As the judging proceeded, the judge asked my competitor and me to

Winning his second Best in Show under Mrs. Robert Lindsay, Joey was handled by Charles Deer at the Longshore-Southport Kennel Club on June 11, 1972.

step to ring center. The handler urged his dog on to go for Joey; immediately Joey bristled up, every hair erect, tail and ears up—he looked magnificent. Joey took a few steps toward his opponent who quickly drew back, running around his handler's legs entwining him with the leash. Loud laughs from the spectators and quick action from the judge to place Joey Best of Breed.

My dear friend Beth and I would go on show circuits together. Being away from home schedules, Joey played games with us at the motel. He would sniff his dish and walk away from his regular food. We did not want him to lose weight from his 17 pounds so bacon at 60 cents a slice was thought a temptation. After a few sniffs, he went to his own dish and finished. He repeated this game with chicken obtained by bribing

Joey's third Best in Show was at the Chenango Valley Kennel Club under the expert handling of Charles Deer on October 15, 1972. The judge on this prestigious occasion was Gerhardt Plaga.

the chef to cook after closing hours. Joey gave it two sniffs and again rejected it. He just wanted to be sure he would make me give him a choice. When important, however, he was completely obedient and cooperative. One time, Beth had a male on the circuit with

Joey and me—we always had a couple of bitches along. Neither male slept in crates. We worried about allowing two males loose so we put leashes on them and placed the other end over our wrists, and the four of us went to bed. When we awakened in the morning, the two males were sleeping soundly cuddled up together!

An uncanny ability, perhaps inherited from grandfather Wagger, Joey instinctively would know young potential show males. To them he was demonstratively bossy, but if he just ignored a young male, it was a sure thing that that youngster would never see the inside of a show ring. A reliable stud dog, though he never bothered bitches around him, Joey proved that being a well-behaved rather spoiled one in the house in no way detracts from show ring ability.

He definitely knew when he won top places by displaying added exuberance. Once when I was showing him in the finale, I shall always remember remarks of three youngsters at ringside: "Which one do you think will win Best in Show?" "The Collie, of course, if the Aussie drops dead!"

That was the time when I was too jittery to handle well. I said to Joey, "You are on your own now, my boy." I am sure he understood. He did everything perfectly.

Handled to his fourth and final Best in Show, this time by owner Mrs. Fox, Joey wins at the Ozarks Kennel Club under Robert C. Graham on September 8, 1974.

In 1978, Joey left this world, taking part of me with him. His presence enriched his breed's prestige, both in distinguished offspring and in demonstrating that an Australian Terrier could win top place, not just now and again, but consistently. He drew admiration from professional handlers, also experienced and novice fanciers from other breeds, as well as his own. There would be frequent remarks on his effervescent personality and his magnificent appearance and his overall correctness.

Much has been written on what ranks a dog among the "Great Ones." Generally accepted is that he must present a glowing, sparkling presence displaying camaraderie which conveys mutual kinship, an incomparable magnetism between dog and man. Also,

Joey's legend lives on in his progeny: Ch. Plesantpastures Ma's Jason, ROM, born on March 2, 1981, is the sire of many champions. Owned and bred by Mrs. Fox.

he must be an unfailing showman, attracting attention immediately upon entering the ring. Of course, besides these qualities is required the fundamental features called for in the breed standard. What else distinguishes a truly great dog: yes, indeed, what Joey possessed—class and charisma.

Over the years I have loved and been loved by many dogs. Each has his or her own special place in my heart and memory. With me Joey's unique place remains undiminished. This is true also of all who knew him. His name conjures recollections of a master dog who incorporated all of the qualities which breeders and exhibitors dream to attain—a dream that materialized in Joey!

OFFICIAL STANDARD FOR THE AUSTRALIAN TERRIER

General Appearance—A small, sturdy, medium-boned working terrier, rather long in proportion to height with pricked ears and docked tail. Blue and tan, solid sandy or solid red in color, with harsh-textured

Ch. Sprite Lea Jordan, ROM (by Aus-Am. Ch. Taralee Sekeluter, ROM out of Ch. Sprite Lea Frederica, ROM), owned by Sprite Lea Kennels.

outer coat, a distinctive ruff and apron, and a soft, silky topknot. As befits their heritage as versatile workers, Australian Terriers are sound and free moving with good reach and drive. Their expression keen and intelligent; their manner spirited and self-assured.

The following description is that of the ideal Australian Terrier. Any deviation from this description must be penalized to the extent of the deviation.

Am-Can. Ch. O'Dare's Wak-A-Bout is a Group-placing red bred by Jean Vander Velden. The judge on this occasion is Aussie expert Mrs. Lenora Riddle.

Size, Proportion, Substance—*Size*—Height 10—11 inches at the withers. Deviation in either direction is to be discouraged. *Proportion*—The body is long in proportion to the height of the dog. The length of back from withers to the front of the tail is approximately 1—1 inches longer than from withers to the ground. *Substance*—Good working condition, medium bone, correct body proportions, symmetry and balance determine proper weight.

Head—The head is long and strong. The length of the muzzle is equal to the length of the skull. *Expression*—Keen and intelligent. *Eyes*—Small, dark brown to black (the darker the better), keen in expression, set well apart. Rims are black, oval in shape. *Faults:* Light-colored or protruding eyes. *Ears*—Small, erect and pointed; set high on the skull yet well apart, carried erect without any tendency to flare obliquely off the skull. **Skull**—Viewed from the front or side is long and flat, slightly longer than it is wide and full between the eyes, with slight but definite stop. **Muzzle**—Strong and powerful with slight fill under the eyes. The jaws are powerful. **Nose**—Black. A desirable breed characteristic is an inverted V-shaped area free of hair extending from the nose up the bridge of the muzzle, varying in length in the mature dog. **Lips**—Tight and dark brown- or black-rimmed. **Bite**—Scissors with teeth of good size.

Neck, Topline, Body—**Neck**—Long, slightly arched and strong, blending smoothly into well laid back shoulders. **Topline**—Level and firm. **Body**—The body is of sturdy structure with ribs well-sprung but not rounded, forming a chest reaching slightly

Ch. Tineetown Talented winning Best in Show at the Sooner State Kennel Club under judge Lenora Riddle. Owner, Mrs. B. McCracken-Purvis.

below the elbows with a distinct keel. The loin is strong and fairly short with slight tuck-up. **Faults:** Cobbiness, too long in loin. **Tail**—Set on high and carried erect at a twelve to one o'clock position, docked in balance with the overall dog leaving slightly less than one half, a good hand-hold when mature.

Forequarters—**Shoulders**—Long blades, well laid back with only slight space between the shoulder blades at the withers. The length of the upper arm is comparable to the length of the shoulder blade. The angle between the shoulder and the upper arm is 90

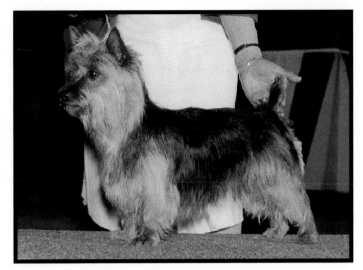

Am-Can. Ch. Plesantpastures One and Only, a Joey grandson, owned and handled by Mrs. M. Goromley.

degrees. **Faults:** Straight, loose and loaded shoulders. **Elbows**—Close to the chest. **Forelegs**—Straight, parallel when viewed from the front; the bone is round and medium in size. They should be set well under the body, with definite body overhang (keel) before them when viewed from the side. **Pasterns**—Strong, with only slight slope. **Fault:** Down on pasterns. **Dewclaws**—Removed. **Feet**—Small, clean, catlike; toes arched and compact, nicely padded turning neither inward nor outward. **Nails**—Short, black and strong.

Hindquarters—Strong; legs well angulated at the stifles and hocks, short and perpendicular from the hocks to the ground. Upper and lower thighs are well muscled. Viewed from behind the rear legs are straight from the hip joints to the ground and in the same plane as the forelegs. **Faults:** Lack of muscular development or excessive muscularity. **Feet**—(See under Forequarters.)

Ch. Seadog's Rosie O'Grady showing off her gait in the ring. Owner, Mary M. O'Connell.

Coat—*Outer Coat*——Harsh and straight; 2 inches all over the body except the tail, pasterns, rear legs from the hocks down, and the feet which are kept free of long hair. Hair on the ears is kept very short. *Undercoat*—Short and soft. *Furnishings*—Softer

Kilgarvan Barnaby Blue, CDX at age 11. Owner, Susan Saulvester.

than body coat. The neck is well furnished with hair, which forms a protective ruff blending into the apron. The forelegs are slightly feathered to the pasterns. *Topknot*—Covering only the top of the skull; of finer and softer texture than the rest of the coat.

Color and Markings—*Colors:* Blue and tan, solid sandy and solid red. *Blue and tan*—Blue: dark blue, steel-blue, dark gray-blue, or silver-blue. In silver-blues, each hair carries blue and silver alternating with the darker color at the tips. Tan markings (not sandy or red), as rich as possible, on face, ears, underbody, lower legs and feet, and around vent. The richer the color and more clearly defined the better. *Topknot*—Silver or a lighter shade than head color. *Sandy or Red*—Any shade of solid sandy or solid red, the clearer the better. *Topknot*—Silver or a lighter shade of body coat. *Faults:* All black body coat in the adult dog. Tan smut in the blue portion of the coat, or

Ch. Tineetown Takiniteeze of Plesantpastures, bred by Pat Connor, imported by owner Mrs. Fox and handled by Peter Green.

dark smut in sandy/red coated dogs. In any color, white markings on chest or feet are to be penalized.

Gait—As seen from the front and from the rear, the legs are straight from the shoulder and hip joints to the pads, and move in planes parallel to the centerline of travel. The rear legs move in the same planes as the front legs. As the dog moves at a faster trot, the front and rear legs and feet may tend to converge toward the centerline of travel, but the legs remain straight even as they flex or extend. Viewed from the side, the legs move in a ground-covering stride. The rear feet should meet the ground in the same prints as left by the front feet, with no gap between them. Topline remains firm and level, without bounce.

Temperament—The Australian Terrier is spirited, alert, courageous, and self-confident, with the natural aggressiveness of a ratter and hedge hunter; as a companion, friendly and affectionate. *Faults:* Shyness or aggressiveness toward people.

Approved August 9, 1988

YOUR AUSSIE PUPPY'S NEW HOME

Before actually collecting your puppy, it is better that you purchase the basic items you will need in advance of the pup's arrival date. This allows you more opportunity to shop around and ensure you have exactly what you want rather than having to buy lesser quality in a hurry.

It is always better to collect the puppy as early in the day as possible. In most instances this will mean that the puppy has a few hours with your family before it is time to retire for his first night's sleep away from his former home.

If the breeder is local, then you may not need any form of box to place the puppy in when you bring him home. A member of the family can hold the pup in his lap—duly protected by some towels just in case the puppy becomes car sick! Be sure to advise the breeder at what time you hope to arrive for the puppy, as this will obviously influence the feeding of the pup

Two Aussie puppies from the author's Pleasant Pastures Kennels ready to meet their new owners.

Seadog's Sailor's Delight, "Austy," at six months. Owned by Mary M. O'Connell.

that morning or afternoon. If you arrive early in the day, then they will likely only give the pup a light breakfast so as to reduce the risk of travel sickness.

If the trip will be of a few hours duration, you should take a travel crate with you. The crate will provide your pup with a safe place to lie down and rest during the trip. During the trip, the puppy will no doubt wish to relieve his bowels, so you will have to make a few stops. On a long journey you may need a rest yourself, and can take the opportunity to let the puppy get some fresh air. However, do not let the puppy walk where there may have been a lot of other dogs because he might pick up an infection. Also, if he relieves his bowels at such a time, do not just leave the feces where they were dropped. This is the height of irresponsibility. It has resulted in many public parks and other places actually banning dogs. You can purchase poop-scoops from your pet shop and should have them with you whenever you are taking the dog out where he might foul a public place.

Your journey home should be made as quickly as possible. If it is a hot day, be sure the car interior is amply supplied with fresh air. It should never be too hot or too cold for the puppy. The pup must never be placed where he might be subject to a draft. If the journey requires an overnight stop at a motel, be aware that other guests will not appreciate a puppy crying half the night. You must regard the puppy as a baby and comfort him so he does not cry for long periods. The worst thing you can do is to shout at or smack him. This will mean your relationship is off to a really bad start. You wouldn't smack a baby, and your puppy is still very much just this.

Roar-Hide® is completely edible and is high in protein (over 86%) and low in fat (less than one-third of 1%). Unlike common rawhide, it is safer, less messy, and more fun for your Aussie.

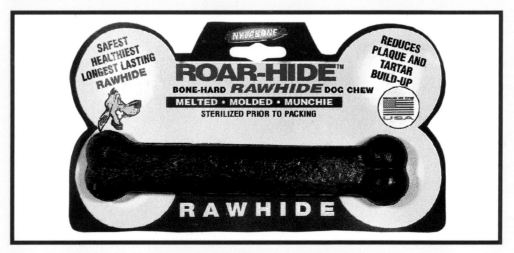

ON ARRIVING HOME

By the time you arrive home the puppy may be very tired, in which case he should be taken to his sleeping area and allowed to rest. Children should not be allowed to interfere with the pup when he is sleeping. If the pup is not tired, he can be allowed to investigate his new home—but always under your close supervision. After a short look around,

When Aussie pups are as adorable as this, choosing one is guaranteed no easy task.

the puppy will no doubt appreciate a light meal and a drink of water. Do not overfeed him at his first meal because he will be in an excited state and more likely to be sick.

Although it is an obvious temptation, you should not invite friends and neighbors around to see the new arrival until he has had at least 48 hours in which to settle down. Indeed, if you can delay this longer then do so, especially if the puppy is not fully vaccinated. At the very least, the visitors might introduce some local bacteria on their clothing that the puppy is not immune to. This aspect is always a risk when a pup has been moved some distance, so the fewer people the pup meets in the first week or so the better.

THE FIRST NIGHT

The first few nights a puppy spends away from his mother and littermates are quite traumatic for him. He will feel very lonely, maybe cold, and will certainly miss the heartbeat of his siblings when sleeping. To help overcome his loneliness it may help to place a clock next to his bed—one with a loud tick. This will in some way soothe him, as the clock ticks to a rhythm not dissimilar from a heart beat. A cuddly toy may also help in the first few weeks. A dim nightlight may provide some comfort to the puppy, because his eyes will not yet be fully able to see in the dark. The puppy may want to leave his bed for a drink or to relieve himself.

If the pup does whimper in the night, there are two things you should not do. One is to get up and chastise him, because he will not understand why you are shouting at him; and the other is to rush to comfort him every time he cries because he will quickly realize that if he wants you to come running all he needs to do is to holler loud enough!

Give the new pup his necessary time to unwind in his new home. Provide a special place that your Aussie can call his own. This is Vixie, owned by Seadog Kennels.

By all means give your puppy some extra attention on his first night, but after this quickly refrain from so doing. The pup will cry for a while but then settle down and go to sleep. Some pups are, of course, worse than others in this respect, so you must use balanced judgment in the matter. Many owners take their pups to bed with them, and there is certainly nothing wrong with this.

The pup will be no trouble in such cases. However, you should only do this if you intend to let this be a permanent arrangement, otherwise it is hardly fair to the puppy. If you have decided to have two puppies, then they will keep each other company and you will have few problems.

If your Aussie breeder has raised her pups in the home, they will have the advantage of some housetraining as well as understanding some basic rules of indoor living.

HOUSETRAINING

Undoubtedly, the first form of training your puppy will undergo is in respect to his toilet habits. To achieve this you can use either newspaper, or a large litter tray filled with soil or lined with newspaper. A puppy cannot control his bowels until he is a few months old, and not fully until he is an adult. Therefore you must anticipate his needs and be prepared for a few accidents. The prime times a pup will urinate and defecate are shortly after he wakes up from a sleep, shortly after he has eaten, and after he has been playing awhile. He will usually whimper and start searching the room for a suitable place. You must quickly pick him up and place him on the newspaper or in the litter tray. Hold him in position gently but firmly. He might jump out of the box without doing anything on the first one or two occasions, but if you simply repeat the procedure every time you think he wants to relieve himself then eventually he will get the message.

When he does defecate as required, give him plenty of praise, telling him what a good puppy he is. The litter tray or newspaper must, of course, be cleaned or replaced after each use—puppies do not like using a dirty toilet any more than you do. The pup's toilet can be placed near the kitchen door and as he gets older the tray can be placed outside while the door is open. The pup will then start to use it while he is outside. From that time on, it is easy to get the pup to use a given area of the yard.

Many breeders recommend the popular alternative of crate training. Upon bringing the pup home, introduce him to his crate. The open wire crate is the best choice, placed in a restricted, draft-free area of the home. Put the pup's Nylabone® and other favorite toys in the crate along with a wool blanket or other suitable bedding. The puppy's natural cleanliness instincts prohibit him from soiling in the place where he sleeps, his crate. The puppy should be allowed to go in and out of the open crate during the day, but he should sleep in the crate at the night and at other intervals during the day. Whenever the pup is taken out of his crate, he should be brought outside (or to his newspapers) to do his business. Never use the crate as a place of punishment. You will see how quickly your pup takes to his crate, considering it as his own safe haven from the big world around him.

A variety of high-quality dog bones are manufactured by Nylabone®. The Plaque Attacker™ Dental Device has raised "dental tips" to reduce tartar build-up on your Aussie's teeth.

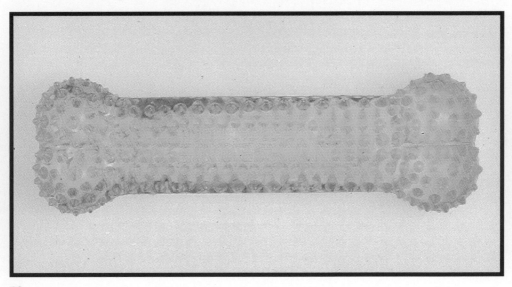

Enjoying a sunny afternoon are Ch. Frederick Willie Wombat, CD and his son Ch. Tak-A-Chance Nip 'N Tucker, owned by Susan Saulvester

GROOMING YOUR AUSTRALIAN TERRIER

EQUIPMENT

If you brush and comb your Australian Terrier regularly—every day if possible—you will find he sheds very little. Use a comb with teeth wide enough apart not to comb out the undercoat. Use a brush of natural bristles, not wire or nylon, to avoid irritating the skin or pulling out the undercoat. *No clippers should ever be used.*

Ch. Plesantpastures Tak-A-Chance, CD, owned by Susan Saulvester, has time to smell the daisies between obedience trials. Always check your Aussie for ticks and fleas after she has explored the great outdoors.

METHOD OF GROOMING

Naturally, grooming for the show ring requires more detail than just keeping your pet in attractive condition; however, grooming not only conceals weaknesses and emphasizes good points legitimately but also improves a dog hygienically and artistically. Far less coat care is needed for the Aussie than for most

Whether a show dog or just a beloved pet, an Aussie should be groomed to look like an Aussie! Some basic technique and the proper equipment will help you keep your Aussie looking his very best. Owner, Esther C. Krom.

other terriers. The coat and its condition varies a great deal with each specimen. Bitches frequently lose their coats after puppies are weaned. For top condition it may be well to take off "dead" coat using your fingers and a stripping knife, never scissors or clippers. Use a medium stripping knife for this. Scissors may be used to keep feet neat and to tidy the tail, underneath, and underparts. These and other canine accessories are best bought from your pet shop, where quality pet supplies are sold. Grooming procedures are more important for show specimens, though some owners prefer even a "pet" specimen to look its best at all times. Little more than brushing and combing are needed for the average pet, plus an occasional tidying

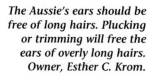

The Aussie's ears should be free of long hairs. Plucking or trimming will free the ears of overly long hairs. Owner, Esther C. Krom.

up. Some coats never seem to need stripping. The following eight steps in grooming are helpful, whether for exhibiting or just to have your dog look his best.

1. **Ears:** Trim ears very close. Ears should be free of long hairs.

2. **Neck:** Trim neck to blend into sloping, well-laid-back shoulders. Shoulders should blend into body.

3. **Tail:** Slim down to body, leaving little hair beyond tip (unless tail is docked too short); if tail is long, blend with back hair.

4. **Coat:** The standard calls for about a two-inch coat. Brush with a stiff brush straight from neck to stern, no parting, then downward over shoulders and rump. Finish with horsehair grooming glove and comb.

5. **Topknot:** Never flatten topknot; train up with brush and fine comb; keep soft by brushing with rain water and coconut oil occasionally (the latter not after pre-show bath). Brush upward just before showing.

6. **Face:** Trim off long surplus hairs; clipping of feelers optional. Clear under eyes slightly to enhance expression. Pluck hair between eyes. Brush muzzle forward.

7. **Ruff:** Brush with outward stroke from under throat to shoulders to cultivate bib-like ruff. Brush chest down to form apron.

8. **Legs, Feet:** Strip off shagginess, back, front, and inside. Use scissors on feet. After trimming close, remove long, light, silky hair. Trim front legs from pasterns down; trim close from hock joint down. File claws. Clean under tail and underparts.

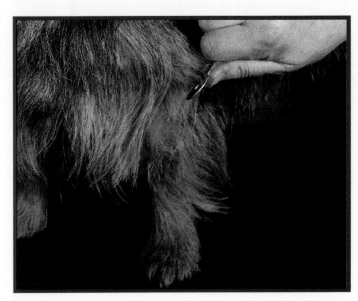

The front legs should be stripped of shagginess, trimming from the pasterns down. Owner, Esther C. Krom.

Mrs. E. Williams suggests the following about grooming an Aussie. She feels that the beginning of spring is a good time to groom your Aussie. It is not necessary to strip him to the skin as this exposes his body, which could become badly sunburnt. In the case of an Aussie, the undercoat should not be stripped out. Nature has provided him with this and no dog should be classed as top notch without it. It is given as a protection and helps to maintain the body's oil. For this reason, too much bathing is not good; it dries up the oil and causes dryness, leading to irritation.

A good stiff brushing and combing each day is a must. Don't scrape with a comb to scratch his skin. Many owners are heavy handed and tear the coat. With a little practice, you can use the comb against your thumb as a stripper to remove the top surface of the coat, which has become dead and very often dingy in color. You will notice in spring time, just as the birds do, Aussies molt (shed), both internally and externally. If the coat is dull and has lost its crispness and he is off his food, check for worms first thing.

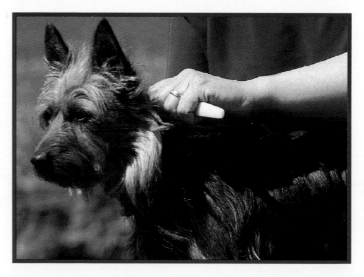

Daily brushing and combing keeps the Aussie looking fresh. Do not be heavy-handed on your Aussie's coat or else you will tear it. Owner, Esther C. Krom.

If regularly groomed, the finger and thumb method can be used readily. The long hair on the ears and near the eyes, the hair that persistently grows near the corner of the eye should be removed by simply plucking out with the finger and thumb. This will grow up across the eye and give your dog a squint, altering his expression. The muzzle and the area between the eyes should be kept free of long hair. Most of this can be done with the finger and thumb process. A stripper or penknife with the serrated edge is necessary for longer, tougher hairs. Scissors should not be used on the ears if it can be avoided, or on the face, as it is dangerous and may give a cut edge look. Long unsightly hair should be removed from around and inside the ear, leaving the ears clean and free from hair, but not taken away from the side or neck as this will spoil the ruff. The face should be kept clean, except from where the topknot starts and grows up between ears. This should be encouraged by brushing both ways with a damp or wet brush. Remove long hair from the corners of the eyes to improve expression. Clean between the eyes to emphasize the stop. Brush and comb his topknot both ways, which can soften by damping but don't leave it ragged—keep it

Sinder, known formally as Ch. Tammikin' Miss Sassy Sinder, sired by Ch. Tinee Town Topman ex Ch. Tammikin's Sweet Wilhelmina, CD. Bred by Shirley Lund and owned by Mae L. Roo.

tidy. The stripper should be used with long straight strokes from the base of the skull down to shoulder level, and eased or graduated so as not to hide the long neck and set of the shoulders. Too much long, thick fur spoils a good setting. They are from the shoulders to the tail onto the back should be done in one long straight strip—not cut in chunks or short stops, giving a choppy look which will grow that way— continuing down the sides and thighs to knee. Too much stripping is undesirable because it does away with the rough coated look that is characteristic of the breed as it was originally known.

The tail should be graduated and studied. Where the tail is inclined to be long it should be blended into the body, and the rest of the tail freed from long hair and clean underneath. A bushy tail not only is untidy but detracts from the appearance of the dog. The hair around the hindquarters should be kept trim and clean, and inside the legs free from long hair. There should be a feather to the knee both front and back, but from the knees down it should be clean, and the feet should be clean, with no long fur between the toes or pads.

Show dogs will be bathed more than pet dogs. This squeaky clean winner is Ch. Shewme's Debrickasaw, owned by Mary M. O'Connell.

BATHING

You should bathe your Aussie as infrequently as possible, and avoid salt water dips. If a bath is necessary for showing, do so about four days before the show. The adult Aussie may go out for a short period in the rain and be dried off with a rough, clean towel. Water and ordinary soaps tend to dry the skin and soften the coat. There are several prepared moist cloths for cleaning dogs available where pet accessories are sold. There are also cleansing fluids and sprays available. Always protect eyes from any product not specified for the eye. Remember that some items are not good for young puppies. Reliable manufacturers spend time and money to label their products to assist you, so read these labels carefully. When purchasing any of the cleansing products and shampoos, emphasize that you do not want any product that will soften the coat. The proper pet products can fulfill your dog's needs far better than products suitable for your own skin and hair care, which can do damage to a dog's coat.

BREED REQUIREMENTS

EXERCISE

Like humans, the amount of exercise required depends on the individual, and like all healthy terriers, Australian Terriers like to run and play outside. However, at no time should they (or any dog) be allowed outside without a leash. A small fenced area is ideal, but an adult Aussie could scale a five-foot fence. Few would go over that height but protection from burrowing underneath is also to be considered. Many a happy Australian Terrier lives long and gaily in cities when given three or four outings of about a half hour each. It is cruel to tie your Aussie outside unless you are working or resting near him.

Patricia Courtney with two favorite Pleasant Pasture champions, Amadeus and Magic Zenda.

SHELTER

Dampness, drafts, and lying on wet ground are bad for most living creatures. Dry cold is less harmful. An Aussie becomes too attached to his family to be kenneled outside. The company of his loved ones is vital to an Aussie, and he is as greedy for love as he is for food.

From about six months of age, an Aussie may run about in light rain for short periods, but never leave him outside except in good weather and in a place where he may have both sun and shade. If he gets wet, dry him with a clean, rough towel. *Never allow your dog to run loose unsupervised.*

Be sure fences and walls cannot be scaled or dug under. Just as soon as your Aussie can understand, and he is wiser than you think, teach him good manners and obedience through the "Three P's": patience, perseverance, and praise.

Though truthfully termed "hardy," your Aussie should be given sensible protection and thoughtful care.

Aussies require fenced yards for their exercise. Be sure the fences can neither be climbed nor burrowed under. Aussies are industrious and too clever for their own good. These two knockabout clowns are Ch. Gladwood's Andrew and Ch. Pleasant Pasture's It's Magic.

CLIMATIC LIMITATIONS

Adaptability of these little terriers to all climatic conditions is proven by definite facts from letters of Aussie owners from Maine to Florida, from the semi-tropical north island of New Zealand to its southernmost tip. There is also no end of evidence that Australian Terriers can live healthily and happily in city or country. Aussies seem to suffer less in warmer localities from bad summer skin conditions than do other terriers. It may be that having originated in a hot climate they have been conditioned to withstand heat better.

TRAINING YOUR AUSTRALIAN TERRIER

Once your puppy has settled into your home and responds to his name, then you can begin his basic training. Before giving advice on how you should go about doing this, two important points should be made. You should train the puppy in isolation of any potential distractions, and you should keep all lessons very short. It is essential that you have the full attention of your puppy. This is not possible if there are other people about, or televisions and radios on, or other pets in the vicinity. Even when the pup has become a young adult, the maximum time you should allocate to a lesson is about 20 minutes. However, you can give the puppy more than one lesson a day, three being as many as are recommended, each well spaced apart.

At about eight months of age, here are Plesantpastures Just Ways and future champion Wags Bac, owned and bred by Nell Fox.

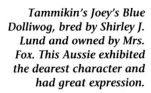

Tammikin's Joey's Blue Dolliwog, bred by Shirley J. Lund and owned by Mrs. Fox. This Aussie exhibited the dearest character and had great expression.

Before beginning a lesson, always play a little game with the puppy so he is in an active state of mind and thus more receptive to the matter at hand. Likewise, always end a lesson with fun-time for the pup, and always—this is most important—end on a high note, praising the puppy. Let the lesson end when the pup has done as you require so he receives lots of fuss. This will really build his confidence.

COLLAR AND LEASH TRAINING

Training a puppy to his collar and leash is very easy. Place a collar on the puppy and, although he will initially try to bite at it, he will soon forget it, the more so if you play with him. You can leave the collar on for a few hours. Some people leave their dogs' collars on all of the time, others only when they are taking the

Am-Can. Ch. Plesantpastures Melba's Echo, bred by Nell Fox and owned by Barbara Deer.

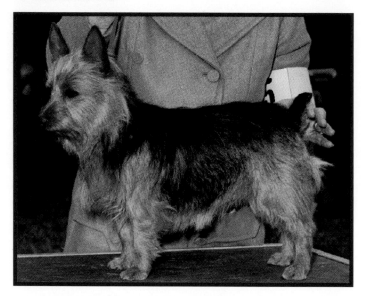

Ch. Plesantpastures Cov Blue Magy, bred, owned and handled by Mrs. Fox.

dog out. If it is to be left on, purchase a narrow or round one so it does not mark the fur.

Once the puppy ignores his collar, then you can attach the leash to it and let the puppy pull this along behind it for a few minutes. However, if the pup starts to chew at the leash, simply hold the leash but keep it slack and let the pup go where he wants. The idea is to let him get the feel of the leash, but not get in the habit of chewing it. Repeat this a couple of times a day for two days and the pup will get used to the leash without thinking that it will restrain him—which you will not have attempted to do yet.

Mrs. Fox handles seven-month-old Plesantpastures Ma's Jenifer and Plesantpastures Jubilee. Both of these youngsters grew up to be champions and produce champion offspring.

Next, you can let the pup understand that the leash will restrict his movements. The first time he realizes this, he will pull and buck or just sit down. Immediately call the pup to you and give him lots of fuss. Never tug on the leash so the puppy is dragged along the floor, as this simply implants a negative thought in his mind.

THE COME COMMAND

Come is the most vital of all commands and especially so for the independently minded dog. To teach the puppy to come, let him reach the end of a long lead, then give the command and his name, gently pulling him toward you at the same time. As soon as he associates the word come with the action of moving toward you, pull only when he does not respond immediately. As he starts to come, move back to make him learn that he must come from a distance as well as when he is close to you. Soon you may be able to practice without a leash, but if he is slow to come or notably disobedient, go to him and pull him toward you, repeating the command. Never scold a dog during this exercise—or any other exercise. Remember the trick is that the puppy must want to come to you. For the very independent dog, hand signals may work better than verbal commands.

Reward your Aussie with a treat. The Carrot Bone™ by Nylabone® is a durable chew containing no plastics or artificial ingredients and it can be served as-is, in a bone-hard form, or microwaved to a biscuit consistency.

THE SIT COMMAND

As with most basic commands, your puppy will learn this one in just a few lessons. You can give the puppy two lessons a day on the sit command but he will make just as much progress with one 15-minute lesson each day. Some trainers will advise you that you should not proceed to other commands until the previous one has been learned really well. However, a bright young pup is quite capable of handling more than one command per lesson, and certainly per day. Indeed, as time progresses, you will be going through each command as a matter of routine before a new one is attempted. This is so the puppy always starts, as well as ends, a lesson on a high note, having successfully completed something.

Call the puppy to you and fuss over him. Place one hand on his hindquarters and the other under his upper chest. Say "Sit" in a pleasant (never harsh) voice. At the same time, push down his rear end and push up under his chest. Now lavish praise on the puppy. Repeat this a few times and your pet will get the idea. Once the puppy is in the sit position you will release your hands. At first he will tend to get up, so immediately repeat the exercise. The lesson will end when the pup is in the sit position. When the puppy understands the command, and does it right away, you can slowly move backwards so that you are a few feet away from him. If he attempts to come to you, simply place him back in the original position and start again. Do not attempt to keep the pup in the sit position for too long. At this age, even a few seconds is a long while and you do not want him to get bored with lessons before he has even begun them.

In the Pleasant Pastures tradition of excellence, here's JoJo owned by Esther C. Krom.

THE HEEL COMMAND

All dogs should be able to walk nicely on a leash without their owners being involved in a tug-of-war. The heel command will follow leash training. Heel training is best done where you have a wall to one side of you. This will restrict the puppy's lateral movements, so you only have to contend with forward and backward situations. A fence is an alternative, or you can do the lesson in the garage. Again, it is better to do the lesson in private, not on a public sidewalk where there will be many distractions.

With a puppy, there will be no need to use a choke collar as you can be just as effective with a regular

Plesantpastures Accent o' Red, placed at the 1980 Westminster show under Peter Kroop. She is by Ch. Plesantpastures Regal Salute, ROM ex Ch. Plesantpastures Fair Acacia, and is bred and owned by Mrs. Fox.

one. The leash should be of good length, certainly not too short. You can adjust the space between you, the puppy, and the wall so your pet has only a small amount of room to move sideways. This being so, he will either hang back or pull ahead—the latter is the more desirable state as it indicates a bold pup who is not frightened of you.

Hold the leash in your right hand and pass it through your left. As the puppy moves ahead and strains on the leash, give the leash a quick jerk backwards with your left hand, at the same time saying "Heel." The position you want the pup to be in is such that his chest is level with, or just behind, an imaginary line from your knee. When the puppy is in this position, praise him and begin walking again, and the whole exercise will be repeated. Once the puppy begins to get the message, you can use your left hand to pat the side of your knee so the pup is encouraged to keep close to your side.

It is useful to suddenly do an about-turn when the pup understands the basics. The puppy will now be behind you, so you can pat your knee and say "Heel." As soon as the pup is in the correct position, give him lots of praise. The puppy will now be beginning to associate certain words with certain actions. Whenever he is not in the heel position he will experience

Winning the breed at Montgomery Kennel Club, this is Plesantpastures Ma's Jubilee, handled by Roy Holloway and winning under Charles Deer.

displeasure as you jerk the leash, but when he comes alongside you he will receive praise. Given these two options, he will always prefer the latter—assuming he has no other reason to fear you, which would then create a dilemma in his mind.

Once the lesson has been well learned, then you can adjust your pace from a slow walk to a quick one and the puppy will come to adjust. The slow walk is always the more difficult for most puppies, as they are usually anxious to be on the move.

If you have no wall to walk against then things will be a little more difficult because the pup will tend to wander to his left. This means you need to give lateral jerks as well as bring the pup to your side. End the lesson when the pup is walking nicely beside you. Begin the lesson with a few sit commands (which he

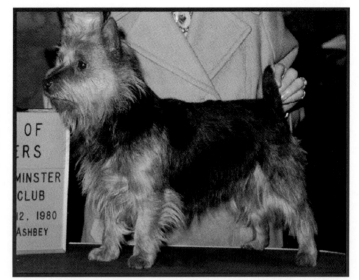

Ch. Plesantpastures Peg O' My Heart, ROM placed at the 1980 Westminster show, handled by Mrs. Fox.

understands by now), so you're starting with success and praise. If your puppy is nervous on the leash, you should never drag him to your side as you may see so many other people do (who obviously didn't invest in a good book like you did!). If the pup sits down, call him to your side and give lots of praise. The pup must always come to you because he wants to. If he is dragged to your side he will see you doing the dragging—a big negative. When he races ahead he does not see you jerk the leash, so all he knows is that something restricted his movement and, once he was in a given position, you gave him lots of praise. This is using canine psychology to your advantage.

Ch. Terrimae Toby, bred by Mae L. Roo and owned by Beth McCracken and Mrs. Fox.

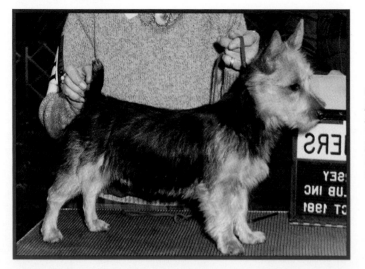

Ch. Plesantpastures T.J. Justin, sired by New Zealand import Ch. Wirrindi Tweedle-Dum, ROM out of Ch. Plesantpastures Jubilee. Owner, Mrs. Fox.

Always try to remember that if a dog must be disciplined, then try not to let him associate the discipline with you. This is not possible in all matters but, where it is, this is definitely to be preferred.

THE STAY COMMAND

This command follows from the sit. Face the puppy and say "Sit." Now step backwards, and as you do, say "Stay." Let the pup remain in the position for only a few seconds before calling him to you and giving lots of praise. Repeat this, but step further back. You do not need to shout at the puppy. Your pet is not deaf; in fact, his hearing is far better than yours. Speak just loudly enough for the pup to hear, yet use a firm voice. You can stretch the word to form a "sta-a-a-y." If the pup gets up and comes to you simply lift him up, place

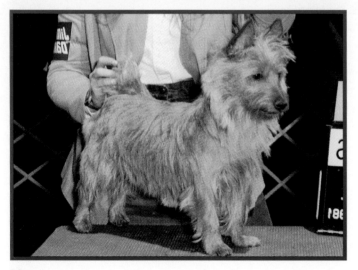

Plesantpastures Keegan at nine months old exhibits all the good points of a red Aussie.

Best Brace in Show, awarded by Josephine Deubler to Ch. Plesantpastures Regency Show and Ch. Regency Plesantpastures Rye, handled by Ida Ellen Weinstock. Owned by Mrs. Fox.

him back in the original position, and start again. As the pup comes to understand the command, you can move further and further back.

The next test is to walk away after placing the pup. This will mean your back is to him, which will tempt him to follow you. Keep an eye over your shoulder, and the minute the pup starts to move, spin around and, using a sterner voice, say either "Sit" or "Stay." If the pup has gotten quite close to you, then, again, return him to the original position.

As the weeks go by you can increase the length of time the pup is left in the stay position—but two to three minutes is quite long enough for a puppy. If your

Ch. Plesantpastures Star Trek, bred by Nell Fox and owned by Barbara Deer.

puppy drops into a lying position and is clearly more comfortable, there is nothing wrong with this. Likewise, your pup will want to face the direction in which you walked off. Some trainers will insist that the dog faces the direction he was placed in, regardless of whether you move off on his blind side. I have never believed in this sort of obedience because it has no practical benefit.

THE DOWN COMMAND

From the puppy's viewpoint, the down command can be one of the more difficult ones to accept. This is because the position is one taken up by a submissive dog in a wild pack situation. A timid dog will roll over—a natural gesture of submission. A bolder pup will want to get up, and might back off, not feeling he should have to submit to this command. He will feel that he is under attack from you and about to be punished—which is what would be the position in his natural environment. Once he comes to understand this is not the case, he will accept this unnatural position without any problem.

Ch. Plesantpastures Wags Bac, sired by Ch. Plesantpastures T.J. Justin out of Ch. Plesantpastures Wags Whim. Bred by Mrs. Fox.

You may notice that some dogs will sit very quickly, but will respond to the down command more slowly—it is their way of saying that they will obey the command, but under protest!

There two ways to teach this command. One is, in my mind, more intimidating than the other, but it is up to you to decide which one works best for you. The first method is to stand in front of your puppy and bring him to the sit

Mrs. Fox handles (Ch.) Plesant Takee Tagsey to first in the Open class at the AKC Centennial Dog Show in 1984 under Aussie expert Charles Deer.

position, with his collar and leash on. Pass the leash under your left foot so that when you pull on it, the result is that the pup's neck is forced downwards. With your free left hand, push the pup's shoulders down while at the same time saying "Down." This is when a bold pup will instantly try to back off and wriggle in full protest. Hold the pup firmly by the shoulders so he stays in the position for a second or two, then tell him what a good dog he is and give him lots of praise. Repeat this only a few times in a lesson because otherwise the puppy will get bored and upset over this command. End with an easy command that brings back the pup's confidence.

The second method, and the one I prefer, is done as follows: Stand in front of the pup and then tell him

Ch. Plesantpastures Magic Lea, placing at the 1984 Westminster show. She is by NZ Ch. Tinee Town Topnotch out of Ch. Black Magical Lester. Bred by Mrs. Fox.

JoJo, owned by Esther C. Krom, is one of Mrs. Fox's favorites of the 1990s.

to sit. Now kneel down, which is immediately far less intimidating to the puppy than to have you towering above him. Take each of his front legs and pull them forward, at the same time saying "Down." Release the legs and quickly apply light pressure on the shoulders with your left hand. Then, as quickly, say "Good boy" and give lots of fuss. Repeat two or three times only. The pup will learn over a few lessons. Remember, this is a very submissive act on the pup's behalf, so there is no need to rush matters.

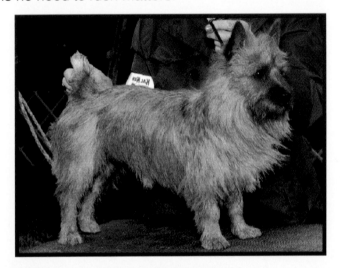

Ch. Plesantpastures Kin O' M'Hart, by Plesantpastures Sunny Kimi out of Plesantpastures Peg O' M' Heart, bred and owned by Mrs. Fox.

RECALL TO HEEL COMMAND

When your puppy is coming to the heel position from an off-leash situation—such as if he has been running free—he should do this in the correct manner. He should pass behind you and take up his position and then sit. To teach this command, have the pup in front of you in the sit position with his collar and leash on. Hold the leash in your right hand. Give him the command to heel, and pat your left knee. As the pup starts to move forward, use your right hand to guide him behind you. If need be you can hold his collar and walk the dog around the back of you to the desired position. You will need to repeat this a few times until the dog understands what is wanted.

When he has done this a number of times, you can try it without the collar and leash. If the pup comes up toward your left side, then bring him to the sit position in front of you, hold his collar and walk him around the back of you. He will eventually understand and automatically pass around your back each time. If the dog is already behind you when you recall him, then he should automatically come to your left side, which you will be patting with your hand.

Plesantpastures T.J. Justin, bred and owned by Mrs. Fox, was sired by Ch. Wirrindi Tweedle-Dum, ROM out of Plesantpastures Ma's Jubilee.

THE NO COMMAND

This is a command that must be obeyed every time without fail. There are no halfway stages, he must be 100-percent reliable. Most delinquent dogs have never been taught this command; included in these are the jumpers, the barkers, and the biters. Were your puppy to approach a poisonous snake or any other potential danger, the no command, coupled with the recall, could save his life. You do not need to give a specific lesson for this command because it will crop up time and again in day-to-day life.

If the puppy is chewing a slipper, you should approach the pup, take hold of the slipper, and say "No" in a stern voice. If he jumps onto the furniture, lift him off and say "No" and place him gently on the floor. You must be consistent in the use of the command and apply it every time he is doing something you do not want him to do.

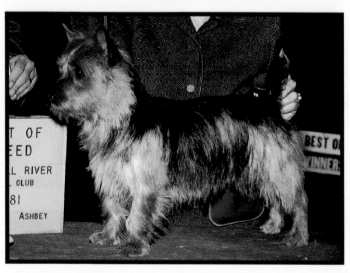

NZ Ch. Wirrindi Tweedle-Dum, ROM, bred and owned by Mrs. Fox, sired many great Pleasant Pastures Aussies.

BREEDING YOUR AUSTRALIAN TERRIER

by Mrs. E. Williams

In choosing a mate for your Australian Terrier dog or bitch, study the standard. Our past benefactors worked hard on this standard on which we are always trying to improve. It is our responsibility to do everything in our power to improve the breed, which is not done in greed or competition, but in the desire to eradicate persistent faults recurring through generations.

Every litter of Australian Terriers should be carefully planned. Breeding requires time, expense and dedication—no matter how cute these little red rascals may seem! Owners, Seadog Kennels.

We have learned from experience that two champions do not often throw champion stock. You may say to yourself, Mrs. So and So has a litter from two champions—they must be good. Remember both sire and dam have a past, and you must pick out a pup from that particular litter as the best of the lot. Since pups develop the faults of past generations, try to be honest and sacrifice. When detecting faults in pups in a litter, sell them only as pets. Yet it is not always possible to detect faults in young puppies, and they are sold in good faith. You can only do your best to protect your reputation by responsible, honest breeding and dealings, and make your pedigrees something to be proud of.

There are breeders who have made a very careful study of inbreeding and linebreeding with great success, and in some case the uniformity of that line is noticeable. I maintain, however, that if this not handled well, the conformation and structure of the animal can suffer. The success of a kennel is not always based on show wins but on its bitches. A bitch may have a good

A kiss for mom...Ch. Plesantpastures Tak-A-Chance, CD, owned by Susan Saulvester.

skull and ear set, may be a little short in foreface and not very strong in bone structure, yet have a good straight front and very few outstanding faults—for such a bitch, I would advise a sturdy dog with all the good points of the bitch but with a good strong jaw. From this mating you may get a litter or some pups worthy of the standard. But if you mate her with a dog with the same faults, all you can hope for is poor stock.

Picking the star puppy from a litter requires an expert eye—even years of experience is sometimes not enough. Your breeder can recommend which pup has the most future "star power."

There are matings that are studied, yet the progeny throw all bad points through past generations of careless breeding. Sometimes these faults do not present themselves until the third and fourth generation.

It is difficult to tell how a puppy will develop. We, in the best of faith, mate two good healthy chosen animals that may result in disappointment, but pity the breeder who attempts to breed two animals with outstanding faults hoping to get one or two good ones. The result of such matings is only the passing of disqualifying or serious faults to future generations.

Like all terrier puppies, Aussies are active, fun-loving and ever alert.

Nine times out of ten when a bitch fails to produce a litter, the owner is all too apt to blame the sire. This is not usually true, and most misses are caused by breeding too early or late or the bitch's lack of fertility. Other causes might be excessive fatness, poor diet, lack of exercise, tumors or cysts, worms or genital infection, incomplete or improper development of sex organs or hormones, or old age.

In Australian Terriers, the mixing of colors can be interesting though not always desirable. For example, a blue and tan mated to a red will often produce a litter of all red or all blue and tan, or sometimes some of each with enhanced color. In such a case, you must watch that the progeny doesn't become streaky or

Puppy colors start to show clearly by a few weeks of age, though the dam seems to recognize the colors in her litter immediately.

shady. We had a red bitch who was mated to a blue and tan, yet she always threw all red, clear lovely color without blemish or smutty markings. Yet her daughter, a rich red, when bred to a blue and tan produced both colors. Surprisingly the bitch took no interest in the blue and tan pups and showed a decided preference for the reds! I have seen throwbacks of generations of one color, yet all at once one pup in a litter will be of a different color. My advice is to keep matings to the same color to avoid smuttiness (which is a fault).

When choosing a pup from a litter, examine the puppy thoroughly for faults, such as over or undershot jaw, allowing for the fact that the pup has only his first baby teeth. Even then you can see whether the pup's jaws is correct. His eyes should be dark, nose black and ears pointed, which will probably not be erect by this age, but they should not stick out from the side of the head. During the teething period, the ears invariably drop but they should at all times be leathery and firm, not soft.

Puppies, of course, will not have the characteristic trimmings or furnishings, but the soft lighter colored hair on top of the head is often discernible. The blue-black and tans are usually black at this stage, but the coat should show promise of lighter color near the body and be of good depth. Even at the puppy stage,

An ex pen situated on an outdoor patio in warm weather is an excellent way to socialize the new Aussie litter. Owners, Seadog Kennels.

reds preferably should be of a clear color, but sometimes they have a darker streak down the back, which gradually disappears with grooming.

Look for a flat skull with good width between the ears. You should already be able to see whether he has good straight front legs and a firm sound body. A good firm body with a straight topline is the best choice. Breeding is a rewarding venture, but always keep the good of the "Grand Little Dogs" first.

Ch. Feathertop Riproarious, known as Rusty, was sired by Crestwoods Crackerjack out of Ch. Birchrun Cricket. Handled by R.J. Bushey and bred and owned by Nancy and Kenneth Goesch, Rusty is winning a Best in Show under the greatly respected Mrs. James Clark.

Ch. Tinee Town Technique lives up to his name "Bravo" by winning the Breed at Westminster in 1992, handled by terrier expert Peter Green under Charles Foley. The author proudly looks on.

SHOWING YOUR AUSSIE

CONFORMATION SHOWS

As long as you have a dog that measures up to the standard's requirements to a fair degree and possesses no flagrant faults, you can show him. Of course, there are some exhibitors who just cannot show because of personal situations, and others whose dogs are out of condition. Newcomers often become discouraged because they don't win their first time out. Consider again and realize, like in all sports, that exhibiting dogs takes some practice and

Mrs. James Clark awards Plesantpastures Ma's Jubilee Best of Breed at the Rio Grande Kennel Club over 36 entries. Owner-handled by the author.

much patience, and that the satisfaction of winning would lose its thrill if it were earned too easily. Perhaps some exhibitors have read and been told that only the very best specimens should be shown, but that is the opinion of just some people. To be discouraged by being over-critical of your dog would mean very few dogs of any breed would get into the ring. The perfect specimen has never been obtained, and what is tops to some judges is mediocre to others. Also consider that Aussies change and frequently improve as they mature. Of course, it is especially

Ch. Crestwoods Crackerjack, known as Jack, has won 3 all-breed Bests in Show, 10 Specialty Bests and the Breed at Westminster all 3 times entered. Jack has sired at least 55 AKC champions including 2 BIS champions, Ch. Crestwoods Jackson and Ch. Feathertop Riproarious.

exciting if your dog has Group possibilities (wins Best of Breed and progresses to compete for Terrier Group first), but regardless of this you can have fun in the classes and perhaps earn a championship. So give your puppies and your older dogs a chance, and then another, and still many more chances to win a ribbon. Know that in doing so, you are not only competing for your own satisfaction but you are also advancing the Australian Terrier breed, which is one of the lesser known breeds and truly in need of enthusiastic support.

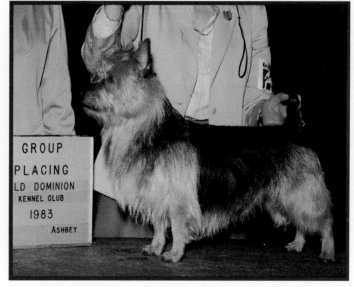

Ch. Samabel Sir Oliver, owned by Alexa Samarotto, is a Group-placing Aussie.

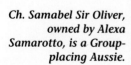

OBEDIENCE & TRAINING
by Barbara Curtis

Training an Australian Terrier in obedience is both fun and challenging. Our Aussies are bright and eager to learn but also easily distracted and always inventive. In my 20 years training Aussies and teaching obedience classes, I've found there are many different ways to teach specific obedience exercises. Most methods will work well if you remember a few basic principles.

First, Aussies respond to positive reinforcement. Using praise and food will get far more out of your dog than a lot of negative verbal and leash corrections. It is especially important to use a lot of praise and encouragement when you begin to teach a new exercise. This does not mean that corrections are not necessary. Once the dog understands what you want him to do and chooses not to do it, or doesn't do it because he isn't paying attention, a light physical correction is in order followed by lots of verbal encouragement and praise as he makes a better attempt to do what you've commanded.

Ch. Gladwood's Andrew R Gladfelter, sired by the great Joey, enjoying a sunny afternoon at home.

Second, all corrections must be non-emotional—a light pop on the leash accompanied by a simple verbal "wrong" works well. Never correct your dog when you are upset or angry. Your emotions will confuse and upset your Aussie, which will then cause him stress. This stress will certainly interfere with his ability to learn and will often cause him to dislike all obedience.

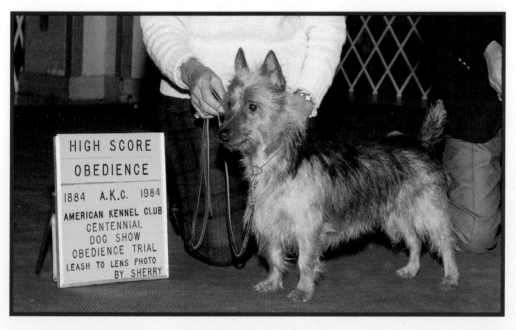

Plesantpastures T'Bac Myrlin, sired by Ch. Gladwood's Andrew out of NZ Ch. Black Magic of Lester, was a high-scoring terrier handled by Tatiana M. Nagro.

This leads to rule number three: Motivation is all important. Terriers get bored with endless repetitions. My Aussies seem to say, "What's in it for me?" I use lots of praise and frequent tasty tidbits to keep their motivation high. I also play lots of games with them during their training sessions (such as keep-away, chase, and retrieving). I have also found that short training sessions are more successful than long ones. I try to quit while things are going well.

I start work with a new puppy by teaching him to come using lots of tidbits and praise. I begin to teach him to watch me by holding tidbits up close to my face and teaching him to catch them when I toss them. I encourage him to walk by my side looking up by holding a tidbit or toy in my hand. I encourage him to retrieve by using a ball or toy tied on a string so that I can help him to bring things back. I want my puppy to love to play so I can use play as a motivator in training. I also take him everywhere with me. The more experiences he has as a puppy, the more easily he will accept new experiences and changes later.

I begin serious obedience between six and nine months by teaching attention. To do obedience well, good attention is crucial. This is especially true with terriers who are so easily distracted. I use Terry Arnold's method of teaching first stationary attention. I then begin heeling, always demanding perfect attention. This can be difficult and slow work, but worth the effort. Once you have good attention, all other obedience work becomes easier. Attention is something you will continue to work on all through your dog's obedience career.

Two other exercises I begin at this time are the "sit in front" and the retrieve. A correct front takes a long time, as the dog must learn to line up his body straight from any angle. I also start the preparation for teaching a force retrieve by giving the dog lots of time to learn to hold and carry his dumbbell.

With attention, heeling, fronts, and retrieving, I begin to introduce a new exercise every week. It is very important to be consistent with your training. Always demand that your dog do every exercise correctly. This is not done by jerking your Aussie around but rather by helping him and using lures as needed to get him to perform an exercise correctly and by rewarding his efforts with lots of praise and encouragement.

Handler Tatiana M. Nagro trains dogs to compete in obedience trials. This Aussie trained by Ms. Nagro easily clears the bar jump.

As your Aussie progresses in obedience, it is important to work him in many different locations. He must learn to handle both stress and distractions. Practice shows, called matches, are essential before he enters the real thing.

When selecting an obedience instructor, or even a training manual, be certain that a positive reinforcement method is advised—this is especially important with Aussies. Equally important, for you and your dog, is that you *have fun!!*

Dancer, trained by Esther C. Krom, shows off his stuff at an agility trial.

AGILITY

by Esther C. Krom

Agility is a sport or performance event consisting of a number of obstacles, various jumps, weave poles, and tunnels designed to test the dog's fitness and physical and mental control. For example, balance is exhibited by negotiating wooden obstacles that are raised above the ground (the A-frame and the dog walk) and a moving obstacle (the see-saw), which requires the dog to reach the moving point of the board and ride it down until the board touches the ground before leaving the obstacle. Touching the contact points of all the wooden obstacles indicates control as well. Also to demonstrate control, a table obstacle is situated on every course and is usually placed somewhere mid-course. The dog, which has been running at a good speed, is expected to reach the table under control and either lay down or sit quietly on it to the count of five before running on to the next obstacle. Suppleness and good condition can easily get a dog through the course in the allotted time, which is measured in seconds.

Agility is a worldwide sport and titles are offered for competition at the various levels. As your dog advances to higher levels of competition, the difficulty of the course becomes more intense with additional turns and obstacles. In the US, agility trials are governed by the rules of various organizations including the USDAA (United States Dog Agility Association), NADAC (North American Dog Agility Council), and the AKC. Anyone interested in specifics of agility rules and regulations should contact one of these national organizations or one of the many local and regional agility clubs.

Aussies, being the "Grand Little Dogs" they are, love the sport. Because of their small size, they do not have the physical balance problems with the contact obstacles that larger breeds may have; however, being "big dogs in little packages," once they are comfortable negotiating the contact obstacles, they think nothing of jumping off without touching the contact points. Therefore, in training, it is best to take it slow, making sure your Aussie hits the contact point for the obstacle every time.

Having great fun, Dancer is doing his thing over the double bar jump. Owner-trainer, Esther C. Krom.

Since agility is a very "up" sport, you should never give your dog corrections. It is praise, praise, and more praise. If you are one of the lucky people owned by an Aussie, you know how much they desire and absorb praise. When on the agilty course you can talk to your dog the whole time. The word "no" is not part of your agility Aussie's vocabulary. You can use the words "leave it" or something similar if your Aussie approaches the wrong obstacle. In training your Aussie for agility, as with some other terriers, it is better not to do it every day. Aussies learn quickly and love the sport, but don't be tempted to rush along—start slow and allow your dog to learn to negotiate the obstacles in a safe, confident manner. Agility is a fun sport, and if you and your Aussie are not having fun, you are doing it wrong!

Sherman, owned by Esther C. Krom of Shastakin Aussies, is growing up nice at ten months of age.

Left: Wattles Plesant Amanda, bred by Beth McCracken and owned and handled by Mrs. Fox. Sired by Aus-Am. Ch. Austrym Optimum out of Tinee Town Tessa. Right: Ch. Plesantpastures Joses Page, sired by Ch. Tinee Town The Page Boy out of Ch. Plesantpastures Ma's Josefin, handled by Mrs. Fox.

Ch. Plesantpastures Chances handled by owner Susan Saulvester with NZ-Am. Ch. Wirrindi Tweedle Dum, ROM handled by Mrs Fox. At nine years of age, Tweedle Dum was the top sire for the breed in 1988.

Ch. Tinee Town Red Halo, bred by Pat Connor and owned by Mrs. Fox, is placing at Boardwalk Kennel Club under the flawless handling of Peter Green.

Ch. Dimonterr Grand Design owned by Irma L. Gibson winning the Breed at the Salina Kennel Club in 1993 under great Aussie advocate Lenora Riddle.

Tineetown Topathshow placing at the 1989 Westminster show. Bred by Pat Connor, handled by Laura Holdren and owned by Mrs. Fox.

Mrs. Fox handles Ch. Plesantpastures Johnathon to Breed win at the Greater Philadelphia show under renowned Australian breeder-judge Pat Connor. Johnathon is owned and bred by Mrs. Fox.

Ch. Registra King Ransom, handled by Andrew Green, does some excellent winning in the late 1990s. Ransom is owned by Mrs. Fox.

ANNAPOLIS KENNEL CLUB

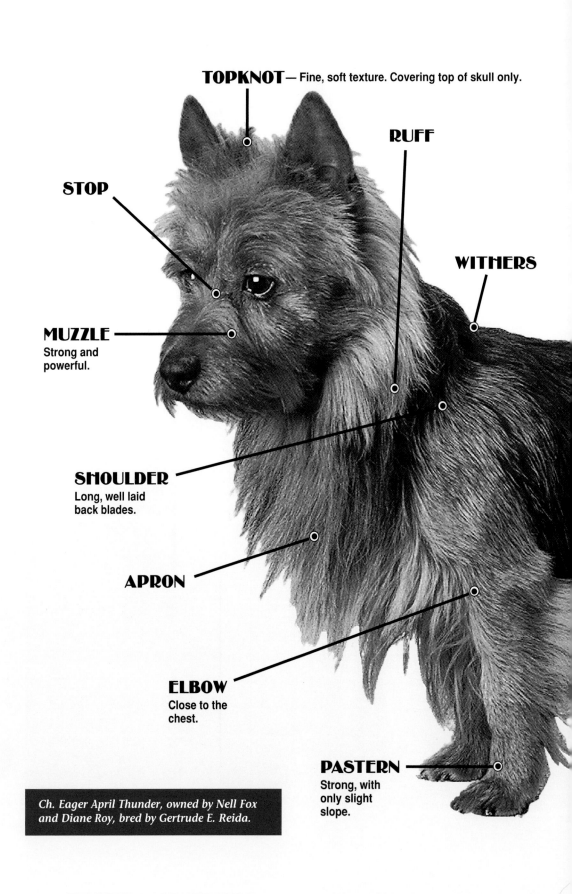

TOPKNOT— Fine, soft texture. Covering top of skull only.

RUFF

STOP

WITHERS

MUZZLE
Strong and
powerful.

SHOULDER
Long, well laid
back blades.

APRON

ELBOW
Close to the
chest.

PASTERN
Strong, with
only slight
slope.

*Ch. Eager April Thunder, owned by Nell Fox
and Diane Roy, bred by Gertrude E. Reida.*